A CHALLENGE OF COMMON KNOWLEDGE I

BARBARA A. PIERCE

A Challenge of Common Knowledge I by Barbara A. Pierce

ISBN 978-1-970072-44-0 (Paperback)
ISBN 978-1-970072-45-7 (Hardback)
ISBN 978-1-970072-43-3 (Ebook)

This book is written to provide information and motivation to readers. It's purpose is not to render any type of psychological, legal, or professional advice of any kind. The content is the sole opinion and expression of the author, and not necessarily that of the publisher.

Copyright © 2019 by Barbara A. Pierce

All rights reserved. No part of this book may be reproduced, transmitted, or distributed in any form by any means, including, but not limited to, recording, photocopying, or taking screen shots of parts of the book, without prior written permission from the author or the publisher. Brief quotations for noncommercial purposes, such as book reviews, permitted by Fair Use of the U.S. Copyright Law, are allowed without written permissions, as long as such quotations do not cause damage to the book's commercial value. For permissions, write to the publisher, whose address is stated below.

Printed in the United States of America.

New Leaf Media, LLC
175 S. 3rd Street, Suite 200
Columbus, OH 43215
www.thenewleafmedia.com

CONTENTS

Four Hundred One Questions and Statements 1

Answer Key 41

Bibliography 61

FOUR HUNDRED ONE QUESTIONS AND STATEMENTS

A Challenge of Common Knowledge I

1. In what country do you live?

2. What is the answer to an addition problem called?

3. How many days are in a week?

4. Which body organ lets you feel heat, cold, or pressure?

5. Pink is made by combining which two colors?

6. Which month is the shortest?

7. H2o is the symbol for which natural element?

8. Which cartoon character is a yellow sponge?

9. A mother with triplets has how many babies?

10. What is paper made from?

11. What is the condition of the atmosphere called?

12. What is the hard outer covering of a tree?

13. What is another name for the human spine?

14. How often does leap year occur?

15. In Roman numerals the letter V represents what number?

16. Fire needs which gas in order to burn?

17. What is another name for frozen rain?

18. Plants produce their own food during what process?

19. Which European country is shaped like a boot?

20. How does an island differ from a peninsula?

21. Who invented the gas mask?

22. Who was the first elected president of the United States?

23. How many permanent teeth does a person have?

24. What kind of sentence shows strong emotion?

25. Thunder is the sound of what?

26. The Great Pyramids are found in which country?

27. What is a family of lions called?

28. How many continents are there?

29. The earth is made up of how many layers?

30. Name the hottest layer of the earth.

31. What punctuation goes at the end of a statement?

32. Which number does the letter X represent in Roman numerals?

33. Name the three primary colors.

34. How many days are in a year?

35. What are body parts and actions that help living things survive called?

36. Birds have two kinds of feathers? Name them.

37. What is the answer to a multiplication problem called?

38. What is the answer to a division problem called?

39. Which two colors make orange when mixed together?

40. Name the thinnest layer of the earth.

41. Is thirty-three an odd or even number?

42. Which is the largest ocean?

43. What is a dried plum called?

44. Name the capital of the United States.

45. Which geometric figure has four equal sides?

46. What are the largest bodies of water called?

47. Name the sign that is used for subtraction.

48. An octopus has how many legs or tentacles?

49. What is a dried grape called?

50. How many wheels does a unicycle have?

51. Canada is in which hemisphere?

52. If you've gotten forty winks, what did you do?

53. How many quarts are in a gallon?

54. When animals sleep all winter they are said to .

55. Name the last letter in the alphabet.

56. What is a baby kangaroo called?

57. If spiders are not insects, what are they?

58. In 1620, the Pilgrims sailed to America on which ship?

59. How many items are in a dozen?

60. Who were the first Americans?

61. How many legs do insects have?

62. Name two types of nutrients found in food.

63. A cube has how many sides or faces?

64. Which planet is called the red planet?

65. What is the name of Charlie Brown's beagle?

66. There are how many letters in the alphabet?

67. Which is the northern most state in the United States?

68. Which is the smallest ocean?

69. What is a three-sided closed figure called?

A Challenge of Common Knowledge I

70. Honey is made by which insects?

71. What is half of a diameter called?

72. Which holiday is celebrated on July Fourth?

73. What should all sentences begin with?

74. What is the hole in the center of an eye called?

75. Scarlet is what color?

76. Name the largest planet.

77. What are the groups called in which whales travel?

78. What is another term meaning cats?

79. Is the tomato a vegetable or fruit?

80. What are animals called that eat only meat?

81. In the process of photosynthesis which gas is released?

82. What is the opposite of a duet?

83. What two colors make green when they are mixed?

84. How many weeks are in a year?

85. Name the thickest layer of the earth.

86. Spiders have how many legs?

87. What are animals called that carry their young in a pouch?

88. What is the colored part of the eye called?

89. What is the smallest known living mammal?

90. What do fish use to breathe?

91. What is your relationship to your cousin's father?

92. Which mammal actually flies?

93. Name the prehistoric animal that resembled the elephant.

94. Name the fastest land animal.

95. What is the frozen form of water?

96. The shape of the earth is a.

97. How many hours are there in a day?

98. Are snakes reptiles or amphibians?

99. How old must a person be to vote in the Primaries?

100. Whose picture is on the five-dollar bill?

101. A fraction represents a part of a.

102. In which month does winter begin?

103. In which city in the United States is the tallest building located?

104. In which direction does the sun rise?

105. Which number is an even number: 21, 72, or 55?

106. What is the hot liquid rock inside the earth called?

107. What part of a plant absorbs water and nutrients?

108. Which teeth are used to grind food?

109. Name the largest bird.

110. Earth gets its heat and light from what source?

111. Which two continents share a common border?

112. The Great Wall of China is on which continent?

113. What imaginary line circles the earth midway between the North and South Poles?

114. Which animal is a rodent: a yak, a platypus, or a gopher?

A Challenge of Common Knowledge I

115. Which sport is played during the Super Bowl?

116. Who invented the telephone?

117. Which instrument do doctors use to listen to heart and lung functions?

118. Pork comes from which animal?

119. What are strong funnel-like winds over land called?

120. Give the month and the day for the start of a new year.

121. How are birds and some insects beneficial to plants?

122. What is the name of the elephant that could fly?

123. If the following words were written in alphabetical order, which would come last: order, equal, or opponent?

124. A quarter and a dime is how much money?

125. What sport is played during the World Series?

126. On which planet do you live?

127. What causes a tsunami?

128. Dairy products are made from which source?

129. How long is four decades?

130. The first Olympic games were played in which country?

131. Who is the caped hero that is said to be, "faster than a speeding bullet"?

132. What do the stars on the American flag represent?

133. What is the largest animal in the world?

134. During respiration animals inhale oxygen and exhale what?

135. Name the ends of a magnet.

136. Which animals are cold-blooded: reptiles or mammals?

137. Are invertebrates animals with or without backbones?

138. Which country introduced spaghetti to the world?

139. What is it called when an animal blends in with its surroundings?

140. Which animal is a mammal: a dolphin or an alligator?

141. Anything that takes up space and has mass is_____?

142. Which organ pumps blood throughout the body?

143. Which body parts help fish move, steer, and balance in water?

144. How many oceans are there?

145. What causes the green color in plants?

146. Where is most of a plant's food made?

147. Name the five Great Lakes.

148. What are the three states of matter?

149. Which instrument is used to measure temperature?

150. In what country is the Amazon Rainforest found?

151. Which is the longest river in the world?

152. The Statue of Liberty stands in which harbor?

153. Is there a physical or a chemical change when wood is sawed into pieces?

154. Which state is a group of tropical islands?

155. Florida is a peninsula. True or False

156. Why did the Boston Tea Party occur?

157. Where does the President live during his presidency?

158. Who was the first black baseball player to play for a major league?

159. Which season follows Winter?

160. How many ounces are in a pound?

161. How many inches are in one foot?

162. What is the name of the giant animals of prehistoric time?

163. Where is the Sahara Desert found?

164. Who wrote the children's books, Charlotte's Web and Stuart Little?

165. Which animals are often referred to as flying foxes?

166. Which state is the largest?

167. According to folklore, what can be found at the end of the rainbow?

168. Which is the highest court in the United States?

169. Columbus claimed America for which country?

170. How many ships did Columbus take on his first voyage across the Atlantic Ocean? Name the ships.

171. Name the two major political parties in the United States?

172. How many feet are there in one yard?

173. Temperature is measured in what?

174. What is a model of our earth called?

175. What period of time can an American President remain in office?

176. Who was the first woman to fly solo across the Atlantic Ocean?

177. The Eiffel Tower is located in what city in France?

178. Conifer is another name for which plants?

179. In June of 1885, the Statue Of Liberty was given to the Empire State by which country?

180. How is the President's wife generally referred to?

181. In the poem, The Night Before Christmas, who is the lead reindeer for St. Nicholas?

182. A leap year has how many days?

183. What term is used to indicate the parts of a whole?

184. Our solar system is in which galaxy?

185. Name the Japanese craft that involves paper folding.

186. Name the path planets take around the sun.

187. What do the fractions 1/2, 2/4, and 3/6 have in common?

188. Which teeth help animals bite and tear meat?

189. What is the shedding of a body covering called?

190. Which animals are called masked bandits?

191. Bats and some whales use sound to find things. What is it called?

192. Which animal builds a dam as a home?

193. What are all the stages in the life of a living thing called?

194. Give a classification for the following: a tux, a cummerbund, britches.

195. Who was the first America astronaut to walk on the Moon?

196. What term is used for the ancient star groupings in the night sky?

197. What are the large wooden carvings of animals, plants, and natural objects that represent a Native American tribe called?

198. Name the national anthem of the United States.

199. Who wrote the song, The Star-Spangled Banner?

200. How many stripes are on the American flag?

201. What country did Columbus think he had found when he reached the shore of San Salvador?

202. What did Columbus call the people he saw in San Salvador?

203. What is another name for the fall season?

204. In which sport is it beneficial to get strikes?

205. Name the Pilgrims' first formal agreement or contract written to establish a government.

206. What are two lines side by side having the same distance continuously between them called?

207. Why did Columbus want to travel to India?

208. What force keeps things from falling off the surface of the Earth?

209. The sun sets in which direction?

210. Is water vapor a solid, a liquid, or a gas?

211. When an animal species no longer exists, it is said to be .

212. What are the prehistoric remains or imprints of plants and animals found in harden rock called?

213. Which is the fastest bird in flight?

214. What year did the first Thanksgiving celebration take place?

215. Name the ceremony in which the President is sworn into office.

216. What is the number above the line in a fraction called?

217. What bony structure supports the body?

218. Which bird is the national symbol of the United States?

219. Name the three kinds of bees found in a hive.

220. Mother's Day comes in which month?

221. What is the number in a fraction below the line called?

222. Give another term for the windpipe.

223. The perimeter of a square is twenty-four inches, what is the measurement of each side?

224. Who is called the mother of the civil rights movement lead by Martin Luther King, Jr. in 1955?

225. What is the term for the regular rise and fall of the earth's bodies of water?

226. Hot air rises and cold air sinks. True or False

227. What body organ is used to detect taste?

228. What is an animal called that hunts another animal for food?

229. What is the smallest part of the body?

230. Father's Day comes in which month?

231. The leprechaun and the shamrock are representative of which holiday?

232. When animals are threaten with extinction, how are they labeled?

233. Name the body system. (Heart, Blood, Blood vessels)

234. Name the body system. (Trachea, Bronchial tubes, Lungs, Air sacs, Diaphragm)

235. The Grand Canyon is located in which western state?

236. Name the river that borders Mexico and the United States.

237. Who invented the electric light bulb?

238. In the Wizard of Oz, what was the name of Dorothy's pet?

239. Which state is the smallest in the country?

240. Name the national memorial that features the massive carved faces of four U.S. presidents.

241. Name the body system. (Mouth, Esophagus, Stomach, Small intestines, Large intestines)

242. What are huge bodies of ice called that slowly move across land?

243. Which volcano erupted in the Cascade Mountains of Washington State on May 18, 1980?

Barbara A. Pierce

244. Give the contraction for will not.

245. Why is March usually the best month for flying kites?

246. Who developed over three hundred products from the peanut and the sweet potato plant?

247. The Thirteen Colonies won their independence from which country?

248. When oxygen and iron combine, rust forms. Is that a physical change or a chemical change?

249. In which story did a wolf try to make a meal of a little girl wearing a red cape?

250. Snowflakes have how many sides?

251. Which four planets are closest to the sun?

252. Who was responsible for such characters as Mickey Mouse, Donald Duck, and Pluto?

253. Rubber comes from what source?

254. Give the name of the woman that designed the American flag for the thirteen colonies.

255. Which is the correct spelling when referring to the building in Washington, D.C. where the U.S. Congress meets: Capital or Capitol?

256. What is it called when an animal resembles another more dangerous one?

257. What is a matador?

258. How many parts does a friendly letter have?

259. What is another name for the buffalo?

260. Two figures that have the same shape and the same size are what kind of figures? (Give a geometrical term.)

261. Who are the two brothers remembered as the fathers of modern flight?

262. Which large luxury liner sank in 1912 after hitting an iceberg in the North Atlantic Ocean?

263. Which metric measurement is used for distance: gram, meter, or liter?

264. What is the distance around the outer edge of a circle called?

265. Water boils at what temperature Celsius?

266. Water freezes at what temperature Celsius?

267. The peacock is the male peafowl. What is the female called?

268. At what temperature Fahrenheit does water boil?

269. At what temperature Fahrenheit does water freeze?

270. What do the annual rings of a tree reveal about it?

271. Who was President during the Civil War?

272. The "I Have A Dream" speech was first orated by whom?

273. Name the three tiny connected bones found in the middle ear.

274. What are three examples of fossil fuel?

275. Images are formed on which part of the eye?

276. In Greek Mythology what term is used to refer to a race of one-eyed giants?

277. How many degrees are there in a right angle?

278. What are the four cardinal directions?

279. What happened when fictional character Pinocchio told a lie?

280. What was the century before this one?

281. Which statement is an oxymoron?

a) Some days are easier than others.

b) The situation got pretty ugly today.

282. What kind of punctuation follows an interrogative sentence?

283. Name the longitude that runs through Greenwich, England, the starting point for longitudes east and west.

284. Which fish has a face that resembles a horse? The male gives birth to its young.

285. What are animals called that eat only vegetation?

286. What is an animal called that eats both plants and animals?

287. Which travels faster, light or sound?

288. What is the letter for fifty in Roman numerals?

289. In which sport are bows and arrows used to hit a target?

290. How many boroughs make up New York City?

291. What are the names of those boroughs?

292. Wolves travel in what type of groupings?

293. Which date is thought by some to be most unlucky?

294. Which author wrote the Harry Potter Series of books?

295. What symbol on a map indicates principal directions?

296. Which mountain is the world's tallest?

297. What is the name of George Washington's home?

298. The book, A Christmas Carol was written by which author?

299. Who was Rip Van Winkle?

Barbara A. Pierce

300. A century is how many years?

301. Name the states that begin with the word 'New'.

302. Which Dr. Seuss character stole Christmas?

303. A field goal in football is worth how many points?

304. What does it mean to be a southpaw?

305. What is a race called that covers over twenty-six miles?

306. Which food gives Popeye super human strength?

307. Mutton comes from which animal?

308. How many zeroes are in a million?

309. What is a person's Achilles heel?

310. What is twelve o'clock in the daytime called?

311. What is twelve o'clock in the night called?

312. How many feet are there in a mile?

313. What is another name for a baby goat?

314. What does the expression 'pull the wool over ones eyes' mean?

315. The Sphinx in Egypt has the body parts of which two mammals?

316. What are animals called that live both in water and on land?

317. Which traditional Japanese wrestling sport takes place in a circular ring?

318. Give the name of the mythological god of the sea.

319. The yellow of an egg is the yoke. What is the white called?

320. Which country has the largest population?

321. Which mathematical operation is used to check division?

322. What flavor is devil's food cake?

323. Name an ancient writing used by the early Egyptians.

324. Which holiday honors America's fallen soldiers?

325. The letters FBI stand for what?

326. The letters UFO stand for what?

327. Which one of the fifty states is the second largest?

328. What is the product of five times eight?

329. Which dinosaur had three horns on top of its head?

330. Which famous entertainer popularized the moonwalk as a dance move?

331. Name the tube and mouthpiece swimmers use to breathe under water.

332. Name the oldest national park in the United States?

333. Ants live in what type of grouping?

334. Nashville is the capital of which state?

335. Which tiny bird is able to hover in mid air while drinking nectar from plants?

336. A scientist who studies plants is call what?

337. The Panama Canal links which two large bodies of water?

338. Name the three main body parts of an insect.

339. What does letter C represent in Roman numerals?

340. Which science deals with the study of the heavens?

341. The digestion of food starts where in the body?

342. Geology is the study of which subject?

343. Is Earth covered mostly by land or by water?

344. Which popular board game allows players to buy and trade real estate?

345. What does the idiomatic expression 'Break a leg' mean?

346. What are dried cranberries called?

347. Which continent has an outline that resembles that of the United States?

348. What is a marionette?

349. Which volcano buried two ancient Roman cities and is still active today?

350. What is the name of the instrument used to measure earthquakes?

351. What is the letter that represents the Roman numeral for five hundred?

352. Name the layer of the atmosphere that is closest to the earth.

353. On film, which colossal ape terrorized New York City by climbing the Empire State Building?

354. How long does it take Earth to orbit the sun?

355. Which artist painted the Mona Lisa?

356. Name the three types of rock found on Earth.

357. What are the five groups of vertebrates?

358. What is the hardest natural substance?

359. A ton weighs how many pounds?

360. If you spent three fourths of a dollar, how much did you spend?

361. Which letter represents one thousand in Roman numerals?

Barbara A. Pierce

362. According to legend, what traditionally happens when groundhog Punxsutawney Phil sees his shadow?

363. Which state is bordered by four of the five Great Lakes?

364. When do nocturnal creatures hunt for food?

365. The Declaration Of Independence and the Constitution were both signed in which city?

366. Which city is home to the Golden Gate Bridge?

367. Which fault line runs through California?

368. The ferocious piranha lives in which river?

369. Harriet Tubman helped slaves escape to freedom by means of a secret system called what?

370. Who were the Code Talkers?

371. Which fleshy fruit has seeds on its surface?

A Challenge of Common Knowledge I

372. What helps the body move?

373. Which animal is said to be man's best friend?

374. Who are the Scandinavians?

375. What part of speech is "wow"?

376. Who was the Shoshone guide and interpreter that accompanied Lewis and Clark on their 1804 expedition?

377. Pearls come from which animals?

378. Which is the longest snake?

379. Who was king of all the ancient Greek gods?

380. What is the root word of disengaged?

381. What goes between the city and state in an address?

382. Name the four intermediate directions.

383. Who developed a code system of dashes and dots that represents different letters of the alphabet?

384. Name the code system of dashes and dots mentioned in # 383.

385. What do the following words have in common? (and, for, or, but, nor, yet, so)

386. Who proved that lightning is electricity?

387. Complete the following analogy. (Wrist is to hand as ___ is to foot.)

388. What does a butterfly begin its life as?

389. How did the Greek warriors gain entrance into the city of Troy which led to the Trojans being captured?

390. What does the expression mean? (Your visit with him was a shot in the arm.)

391. What is the long Japanese robe worn with a sash called?

392. Name the world's largest lizard.

393. Which comet can be seen in the sky every 76 years?

394. What is the plural form of deer?

395. Which giant reptile-like creature is reported to be in one of Scotland's lakes, yet there has been no proof?

396. Name the joint between the leg and the foot.

397. Was William Shakespeare's Romeo and Juliet a comedy or a tragedy?

398. Is a scallion an animal, a plant, or an article of clothing?

399. Why was Alaska called Seward's Folly and Seward's Icebox when bought from Russia in 1867?

400. What is the highest mountain in North America?

401. What's the capital of Alaska?

ANSWER KEY

1. The United States
2. the sum
3. seven
4. the skin
5. red and white
6. February
7. water
8. SpongeBob Square Pants
9. three
10. trees
11. the weather
12. the bark
13. backbone
14. once every four years
15. five
16. oxygen

17. sleet
18. photosynthesis
19. Italy
20. An island is surrounded by water on all sides. A peninsula is surround by water on three sides only.
21. John Morgan
22. George Washington
23. thirty-two
24. exclamatory
25. lightning
26. Egypt
27. a pride
28. seven
29. three
30. the core
31. a period
32. ten
33. red, yellow, and blue
34. three hundred sixty-five days
35. adaptations
36. contour and down feathers

37. product
38. a quotient
39. red and yellow
40. the crust
41. odd
42. the Pacific Ocean
43. a prune
44. Washington D.C.
45. a square
46. oceans
47. the minus sign
48. eight
49. a raisin
50. one
51. Northern
52. slept
53. four
54. hibernate
55. the letter (Z)
56. a joey
57. arachnids

A Challenge of Common Knowledge I

58. the Mayflower
59. twelve
60. the Indians or Native Americans
61. six
62. vitamins and minerals
63. six
64. Mars
65. Snoopy
66. twenty-six
67. Alaska
68. The Indian Ocean
69. a triangle
70. bees
71. a radius
72. Independence Day
73. a capital letter
74. the pupil
75. red
76. Jupiter
77. herds
78. felines

79. a fruit
80. carnivores
81. oxygen
82. a solo
83. yellow and blue
84. fifty-two
85. the mantle
86. eight
87. marsupials
88. the iris
89. the shrew
90. gills
91. He's your uncle.
92. the bat
93. the mammoth
94. the cheetah
95. ice
96. a sphere
97. twenty-four
98. reptiles
99. eighteen

A Challenge of Common Knowledge I

100. Abe Lincoln
101. whole
102. in December
103. New York City
104. in the east
105. seventy-two
106. magma
107. the root
108. molars
109. the ostrich
110. the sun
111. Europe and Asia
112. Asia
113. the Equator
114. a gopher
115. football
116. Alexander Graham Bell
117. the stethoscope
118. the pig
119. a tornadoes
120. January 1

121. They help to pollinate plants.
122. Dumbo
123. order
124. thirty-five cents
125. baseball
126. Earth
127. earthquakes and volcanic eruptions on the ocean floor, also strong winds at the water's surface
128. milk
129. forty years
130. Greece
131. Superman
132. the fifty states
133. the whale
134. carbon dioxide
135. poles
136. reptiles
137. without
138. China
139. camouflage
140. a dolphin

141. matter
142. the heart
143. fins
144. five (Atlantic, Arctic, Indian, Pacific, Southern or Antarctic)
145. chlorophyll
146. in the leaves
147. Lake Erie, Lake Huron, Lake Michigan, Lake Ontario, and Lake Superior
148. solid, liquid, and gas
149. a thermometer
150. Brazil
151. the Nile River
152. New York Harbor
153. a physical change
154. Hawaii
155. True
156. It was a protest against the heavy taxes England placed on tea and other goods sent to the thirteen colonies.
157. In the White House
158. Jackie Robinson
159. Spring

160. sixteen
161. twelve
162. dinosaurs
163. on the continent of Africa
164. E. B. White
165. bats
166. Alaska
167. a pot of gold
168. the Supreme Court
169. Spain
170. three (Pinta, Nina, Santa Maria)
171. the Democratic Party and the Republican Party
172. three
173. degrees
174. a globe
175. eight years
176. Amelia Earhart
177. Paris
178. the evergreens
179. France
180. the First Lady

181. Rudolph
182. three hundred sixty-six
183. fraction
184. the Milky Way
185. origami
186. orbit
187. They are equivalent fractions.
188. canines
189. molting
190. raccoons
191. echolocation
192. a beaver
193. life cycle
194. clothing
195. Neil Armstrong
196. Constellations
197. totem pole
198. The Star-Spangled Banner
199. Francis Scott Key
200. thirteen
201. India

202. Indians

203. Autumn

204. bowling

205. The Mayflower Compact (written aboard the Mayflower, 1620)

206. parallel lines

207. to get silk and spices

208. gravity

209. west

210. gas

211. extinct

212. fossils

213. the falcon

214. 1621

215. the Inauguration Ceremony

216. numerator

217. the skeleton

218. the bald eagle

219. the queen, the drone, the worker

220. May

221. denominator

222. trachea

223. six

224. Rosa Parks

225. tides

226. True

227. the tongue

228. a predator

229. the cell

230. June

231. St. Patrick's Day

232. endangered

233. circulatory system

234. respiratory system

235. Arizona

236. The Rio Grande

237. Thomas Edison

238. Toto

239. Rhode Island

240. Mount Rushmore (in South Dakota)

241. digestive system

242. glaciers

243. Mount St. Helens

244. won't

245. March is a windy month.

246. George Washington Carver

247. Britain

248. a chemical change

249. Little Red Riding Hood

250. six

251. Mercury, Venus, Earth, Mars

252. Walt Disney

253. rubber trees

254. Betsy Ross

255. Capitol

256. mimicry

257. a bull fighter

258. five (heading, greeting, body, salutation, signature)

259. bison

260. congruent

261. Wilbur and Orville Wright

262. The Titanic

263. Meter

264. circumference
265. 100 degrees Celsius
266. 0 degrees Celsius
267. pea hen
268. 212 degrees Fahrenheit
269. 32 degrees Fahrenheit
270. How old it is
271. Abe Lincoln
272. Martin Luther King, Jr.
273. Hammer, Anvil, Stirrup
274. oil, coal, and natural gas
275. Retina
276. Cyclopes
277. 90 degrees
278. north, south, east, and west
279. Pinocchio's nose grew longer.
280. the Twentieth Century
281. b) The situation got pretty ugly today.
282. a question mark
283. the Prime Meridian
284. a sea horse

285. herbivores

286. omnivores

287. Light travels faster than sound.

288. the letter (L)

289. archery

290. five

291. Manhattan, Bronx, Brooklyn, Queens, and Staten Island

292. in packs

293. Friday the Thirteenth

294. J.K. Rowling

295. compass rose

296. Mt. Everest (Himalaya Mountains, 29,028 ft.)

297. Mount Vernon

298. Charles Dickens

299. A fictional character that finally wakes up after sleeping for twenty years (The author of the short story is Washington Irving.)

300. one hundred years

301. New York, New Jersey, New Mexico, New Hampshire

302. the Grinch

303. three points

A Challenge of Common Knowledge I

304. You're left-handed.
305. a marathon
306. spinach
307. sheep
308. six
309. a person's weak spot
310. noon
311. midnight
312. five thousand two hundred eighty feet
313. kid
314. to deceive a person
315. a man and a lion
316. amphibians
317. Sumo wrestling
318. Neptune
319. the albumen
320. China
321. multiplication
322. chocolate
323. hieroglyphics
324. Memorial Day

325. Federal Bureau of Investigations
326. Unidentified Flying Object
327. Texas
328. forty
329. triceratops
330. Michael Jackson
331. snorkel
332. Yellowstone Park
333. a colony
334. Tennessee
335. the humming bird
336. a botanist
337. The Pacific and The Atlantic
338. head, thorax, abdomen
339. one hundred
340. Astronomy
341. the mouth
342. Earth and its composition
343. water
344. Monopoly
345. Good Luck!

346. craisins
347. Australia
348. a puppet controlled by strings
349. Mount Vesuvius
350. a seismograph
351. the letter (D)
352. the troposphere
353. King Kong
354. three hundred sixty-five days
355. Leonardo da Vinci
356. igneous, sedimentary, and metamorphic rock
357. amphibians, birds, fish, mammals, reptiles
358. the diamond
359. two thousand pounds
360. seventy-five cents
361. the letter (M)
362. Six extra weeks of winter can be expected.
363. Michigan
364. at night
365. Philadelphia
366. San Francisco

367. The San Andreas Fault Line
368. The Amazon River
369. The Underground Railroad
370. The Navajo Indians (developed an unbreakable code used during WWII)
371. the strawberry
372. the muscles
373. the dog
374. The people from Sweden, Denmark, Norway, and sometimes Finland and Iceland
375. an interjection
376. Sacajawea (1804-1805)
377. oysters
378. the reticulated python
379. the Greek god Zeus
380. engage
381. a comma
382. Northwest, Northeast, Southwest, and Southeast
383. Samuel F.B. Morse
384. The Morse Code
385. They are conjunctions.

A Challenge of Common Knowledge I

386. Benjamin Franklin

387. ankle

388. a caterpillar

389. Greek warriors built a great wooden horse as a gift to Troy. Unaware of men hidden inside, the Trojans took it into their city.

390. You lifted his spirits.

391. a kimono

392. the Komodo dragon

393. Halley's Comet

394. deer

395. The Loch Ness Monster or Nessie

396. the ankle

397. a tragedy

398. a plant

399. Alaska was thought to be a frozen wasteland by many when Secretary of State William H. Seward bought it.

400. Mount Denali in Denali National Park

401. Juneau

BIBLIOGRAPHY

ABC Of Nature, A Family Answer Book. Pleasantville, NY: Reader's Digest Assoc. Inc. 1988.

Butterfield, Moira. 1000 Facts About The Earth. New York, NY: Scholastic Inc. 1993.

Brent, Lynnette, et al. Children's Illustrated Atlas Of The United States. Rand McNally and Company. 2005.

Falstein, Mark. Meeting The Challenge/ Biographies Of Black Americans. Elizabethtown, PA: The Continental Press Inc. 1987.

Mallinson, George G. et al. Science Horizons. USA: Silver Burdett & Ginn. 1991.

Official Punxsutawney Groundhog Site. (July 7, 2009). About Groundhog Day (Online). Groundhog.org

Rogers, Chester E.A Brief History of the Pilgrims. Plymouth, Mass. The Rogers Print: 1947.

Rosenberg, Matt. (July 12,2009). The Fifth Ocean (Online). About.com

Steele, Philip. Vampire Bats And Other Creatures Of The Night. New York, NY: Kingfisher. 1995.

Taylor, Barbara. Nature Watch Snakes. New York, NY:

Lorenz Books. 1999.

The Eyewitness Visual Dictionaries/The Visual Dictionary Of The Human Body. New York, NY: Dorling Kingdersley Inc. 1991.

The Trojan War, http ://www.stanford.edul-plomiolhistory.html July 9,2009.

www.ingramcontent.com/pod-product-compliance
Lightning Source LLC
Chambersburg PA
CBHW071915070526
44583CB00016B/2003